W9-AOL-196

GOOD MANNERS
during SPECIAL
OCCASIONS

Published by The Child's World®
1980 Lookout Drive • Mankato, MN 56003-1705
800-599-READ • www.childsworld.com

Acknowledgments
The Child's World®: Mary Berendes, Publishing Director
The Design Lab: Design and production
Red Line Editorial: Editorial direction

ISBN 9781614732297
LCCN 2012932442

Printed in the United States of America
Mankato, MN
July 2012
PA02126

ABOUT THE AUTHOR

Ann Ingalls writes stories and poems for people of all ages as well as resource materials for parents and teachers. She was a teacher for many years and enjoys working with children. When she isn't writing, she enjoys spending time with her family and friends, traveling, reading, knitting, and playing with her cats.

ABOUT THE ILLUSTRATOR

Ronnie Rooney took art classes constantly as a child. She was always drawing and painting at her mom's kitchen table. She got her BFA in painting from the University of Massachusetts at Amherst and her MFA in Illustration from Savannah College of Art and Design in Savannah, Georgia. She now lives and works in Fort Lewis, Washington. Her plan is to pass her love of art and sports on to her two young children.

CONTENTS

Special Occasions

What kind of special **occasion** do you like best? Parties and concerts are fun. So are holidays and fancy dinners. You get to **mingle** with other people. And you can eat tasty food. You may see a great show. Or you can hear new kinds of music. Special occasions can be a lot of fun!

But do you know what to do and say at those special events? You need to know when to clap at a concert. And you should know how to eat at restaurants. These are your manners. Good manners help make special occasions even more special!

Dressing Up

Dress clothes are not as cozy as jeans. But you sure do look nice in dress clothes! And looking nice shows that you care about where you are going.

Make sure your dress clothes are clean. Check for wrinkles. You don't want to look like a raisin! Ask a parent to iron your clothes. And wipe dirt or mud off your shoes.

Comb your hair and wash your face. Turn around in front of the mirror. How do you look? You need to look your best for special events!

Weddings

Weddings can be a lot of fun. You can wear your shiny new shoes and best outfit. You will look very spiffy. But how can your manners be spiffy, too?

Sit quietly through the **ceremony**. Do not wriggle and squirm. It might be long. But being quiet shows **respect** to the wedding couple.

At the **reception**, you will meet other guests. Say, "Hello" and shake their hands. Sit nicely

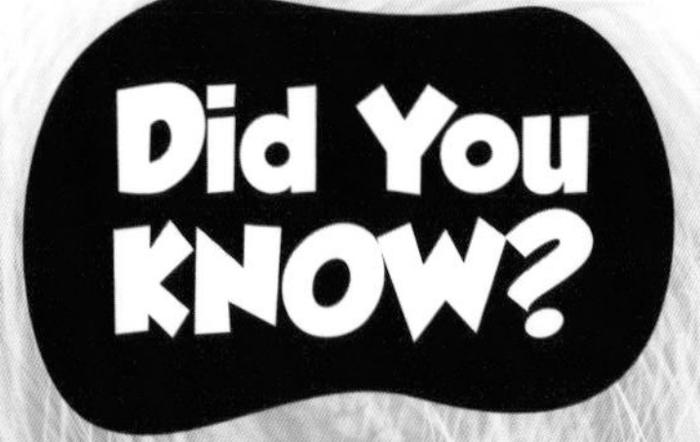

In China, you may sit for a long time at a wedding meal. The meal can have ten or more courses of food.

in your seat at the dinner. Put your napkin in your lap. Say, “Please” and “Thank you.” And don’t throw ice at your cousin Jerry. It does not matter what funny faces he makes!

Fancy Dinners

Going out to eat is a special treat. It might be for a birthday or just for fun. But you need to have certain manners in a restaurant.

Sit at the table. Do not run around. Restaurants are busy places. You might get in the way of a waiter or a diner.

Order your food nicely from the waiter. Listen while the waiter talks with your family. Wait until it is your turn to order. Say, "I would like the salmon, please."

The waiter will set your food on the table. Do not grab the plate. Remember to say, "Thank you."

When eating, chat with others. Ask, "How is your dinner?" But wait until you are done chewing. And when the meal is over, thank your family for taking you out.

Concerts and Shows

It takes a lot of effort to put on a concert or show. Musicians practice songs. Actors practice their lines. At show time, everything comes together. You get to listen to beautiful music. Or you can watch a magical scene from a play.

Show your respect with a few manners. Clap when musicians come on stage. But stop before the music starts.

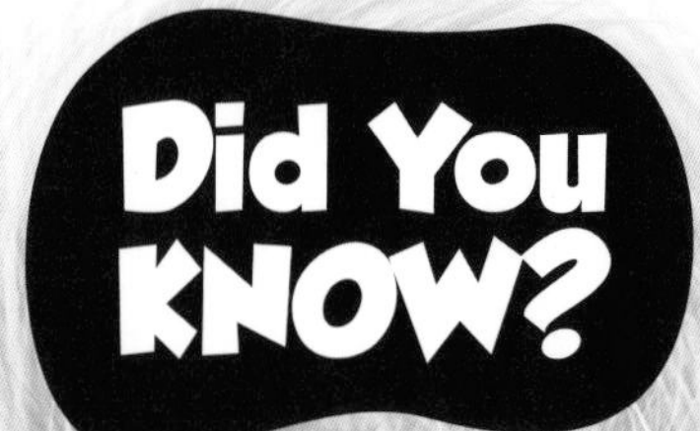

Bravo *is an Italian word. It means "bravely done." You can also say, "*Encore.*" This is French for "do it again."*

Sit quietly in your seat. Listen to the music or watch the play. Look up at the stage. Show respect to the other people in the **audience**.

It is the end of the concert or show. Now is the time to clap loudly. You can even say, "Bravo!" If you are not sure when to clap, watch others to know.

Birthday Parties

It is your special day. And you are going to have a birthday party! Be a good host. Invite guests a few weeks before the party. Give them time to plan. When guests arrive, talk with every person. Thank them for coming. Say, "It was so nice of you to come."

You should be a good guest, too. Tell the host if you can come to the party. At the party, you will have food and drinks. Always say, "Please" and "Thank you." And if you do not like a food, don't say anything. Just try a different food. Play games nicely with others. And when you leave, thank the host. Say, "Thanks. That was a great party!"

Holidays

At the holidays, you get to see your **relatives**. There is lots of good food to eat and fun to have. Help your parents get ready for a holiday party. Offer to set the table. Or ask, "How may I help?"

Talk with relatives. Ask, "How are you?" Guests will know that you are glad to see them. You can even tell some jokes. Your great-uncle Carl will love them!

And you should share your toys with your cousins. Let them play with your new board game. It will be fun for everyone.

Thank You
Thank You

Getting Gifts

Did you get some great gifts? It might be hard to remember who gave you the super soaker. Make sure you write down who gave you what. This way you can thank Aunt Dorothy for the book. And you can thank your friend Reggie for the water toy.

Write thank you notes to each person who gave you a gift. Make the notes special for each person. Name the gift that was given. And write how much you liked it.

A Bit More Polite

Good manners are a bit different in different places. But now you know how to act at any special occasion. You know when to clap at concerts and shows. You know how to eat at weddings and restaurants. And you know how to act at holidays and birthday parties.

Have good manners at those special occasions. It shows that you feel great about being there. Look your best. And don't forget to have a grand time, too!

Put your new special occasion manners in action with this pop quiz! Will you choose the right rules?

Wear your dressy clothes to a special event:

a. even if they smell like pizza.
b. if they are clean and free of wrinkles.
c. under your Halloween costume.
d. only if your jeans are dirty.

When at a wedding ceremony:

a. hum the whole time.
b. shake your legs as fast as you can.
c. listen quietly.
d. whisper to your little brother.

At a restaurant, you should:

a. toss your food at your little sister.
b. run around shouting, "Let's eat! Let's eat! Let's eat!"
c. shout your order when your brother orders.
d. chat with others and enjoy your food.

At a concert, you should:

a. snap your fingers the whole time.
b. dance up and down the aisles.
c. clap when the music stops.
d. stand on your seat.

At birthday parties, you should:

a. ignore the guests.
b. talk with only a few guests.
c. say the food is gross.
d. talk with everyone.

At holiday parties, it is important to:

a. lock up your toys so no one can play with them.
b. sit in the corner and frown.
c. help your parents get ready for the party.
d. only talk to your dog.

Please do not write in the book!

Glossary

audience (AW-dee-uhnss): An audience is the group of people watching a show or concert. The audience is quiet during a concert.

ceremony (SER-uh-moh-nee): A ceremony is the actions, words, and music performed to mark a special occasion. Sit still during the wedding ceremony.

mingle (MING-guhl): To mingle is to mix with other guests at a party. You should mingle with party guests.

occasion (uh-KAY-zhuhn): An occasion is a special or important event. A special occasion is a good time to dress up.

reception (ri-SEP-shuhn): A reception is a fancy party. You can eat a nice dinner at the reception.

relatives (REL-uh-tivz): Relatives are members of your family. Talk with your relatives at your holiday party.

respect (ri-SPEKT): To have respect is to care for another person's feelings or treat his or her home with care. Shaking someone's hand shows your respect.

Web Sites

Visit our Web site for links about manners during special occasions: **childsworld.com/links**

Note to Parents, Teachers, and Librarians: We routinely verify our Web links to make sure they are safe and active sites. So encourage your readers to check them out!

Books

Burstein, John. *Manners, Please!: Why It Pays to be Polite*. New York: Crabtree, 2011.

Eberly, Sheryl. *365 Manners Kids Should Know: Games, Activities, and Other Fun Ways to Help Children Learn Etiquette*. New York: Three Rivers Press, 2001.

Espeland, Pamela. *Dude, That's Rude!* Minneapolis, MN: Free Spirit Publishing, 2007.

Index